MONEY

The system that should be taught in school.

Get your own copy
& Change your future!

Scan the

Q.R. Code Below.

Table of Contents

MONEY

**The system that should be
taught in school.**

INTRODUCTION

The more you get out of this book the more you'll get out of life.

Imagine a very ordinary person between the ages of 17 and 50, living in an ordinary home, on an ordinary street and working in an ordinary place, they most likely work all day only to return home at the end working day, eating tea, sitting on the sofa and then watching tv, then the next day is a repeat of the last.

Only the weekends seem to bring a break to routine of a conveyor belt cycle of life, with a 'Thank *uck its Friday!' said to yourself to celebrate the end of yet another week and even then, not much really happens on that weekend does it, chances are you just spend money you may not have and then have no choice but to go back to work on the Monday, it's just very ordinary life, in Mundane-Ville!

What happened to those dreams when you were young of becoming a superhero, an astronaut or a YouTube millionaire, how did your life turnout like it is now?

But something amazing is about to happen.

YOUR LIFE IS ABOUT TO CHANGE.

FOREVER.

<u>But...</u>

In order for you to get the most out of this content

you must first...

- Decide are you are happy with the money situation you are in right now & your future? If you're not, then you need to get started right now on the road to change.

- Are you strong enough in your mind & have the willpower to change for the better?

- You must be willing to read each chapter twice if you need to, to get the lessons into your new mindset.

- As you read along, remember STOP frequently and really ask yourself this question 'How can I use the information in this section to better my current life? 'By asking yourself this question or writing it down your mind will naturally want to answer it honestly.

- Get a pen or highlighter and highlight or underscore any parts or sections of text that you find most useful, this way you can later on for reference flick though the pages again, but only see the parts that you found interesting, and you felt you really needed to know.

- Do you think you can review sections of this book frequently? Don't just read it once and put it on the shelf, this book is the first step of training yourself to change the way you think and do things, so you must recap the material and go through the content until it becomes 2nd nature to you.

REMEMBER !

If the system, you currently used to be working correctly for you then you wouldn't be investing your time in reading this book would you?

Did you know that even if you maintain a tip-top shape, eat, exercise, and stay healthy, that your life on this planet is only set for a very limited amount of time, your immortality as you think you have it, is nothing more than just as short as a catnap in the eyes of the world?

Yes, according to statistics the average lifespan of a healthy human being is very short indeed,

Did you know?

That you will only exist for around 4000 weeks from the day you were born until you bid adieu.

It's almost like a blink of an eye, so you better start living your best life now enjoy every experience good or bad and make every moment count as you will only exist on this planet for around 4000 weeks!

Another little fact is that let's assume that you start working at 18 and later on your life you make the decision to try to retire early, maybe around 55 years old, just so you can spend your time travelling or enjoying yourself when you still have energy after the kids have left home then you will then only have about 1900 weeks.

Maybe you don't start work at 18, maybe you decide to go into further education after 18 and stay until your 25 and after that then go to work, but if you do this then you only have 1560 weeks of your mortal clock limit left, that's only 1560 weeks to learn everything you need about a trade or skill, and get good enough at it to, grow your self-worth so you can start saving money.

Time is stacked against you on the conveyor belt of life, so look no further!

ABOUT ME...

My Name is Grant and from the age of 25, I was one of the many who worked all day then repeated the process again the next, over and over in what seemed like a never ending cycle, it didn't take long for me to decide that I simply didn't want to live my life this way, I saw wealthy people going on holidays, having nice cars and having nice things and I wanted to be like them and I was rapidly getting fed up of looking at how much change I had in my pocket and letting that decide for me what I was going to buy for lunch.

The worst part of it was that at work there was always this old person at work that we always had to hear in the background as they moaned about how bad things are but I knew this person would work in a place they hated till they were 65 then retire if they didn't die first and most likely do noting with their lives retiring as they were just too miserable to suddenly do anything with what was left of their life, if I wasn't careful this would be me getting slowly beaten down by the system and fast forward 40 years and I would be the old man moaning, this was definitely wasn't going to be my story for the way I would spend the rest of my life, so I had to change it quickly or fail in the attempt but I had to try to get out of this situation.

I left my job and travelled, I had many different jobs and learn from many mentors that I met along my path through life, the lessons they taught me changed my life, some gave good advice and some not, but rule of thumb is follow and learn from someone who is successful and copy what they do, it's a blueprint for your own success.

The lessons good and bad have been the foundation of everything that I have managed to achieve, I teach them to my friends and my family as it's my mission to pass this information onto as many people as I can to help them escape the normal drone mentality of working for a company that doesn't really value you. I want to share what I have been taught with you and teach you how to beat the system and live your best life!

Money... 'The system that should be taught in school' is a book about teaching you the process and system that will allow you have enough money, while you are young and energetic enough to enjoy it and to do things you like, the current system that everyone is taught by the news, the schools and the government fails you on so many levels, this is why so many people are in debt and just get further into it with no escape, then they have to work in a job they hate for the rest of your lives in the hope they may be able to retire one day, with a little bit of money to enjoy in their old age, but the truth is...that's **'THE TRAP'**..it is just a dream told to you and put into your mind and you need to be asleep to believe it!

The only person who will look after you…. is you…. its not the government, your pension or anything like that,

YOU MUST TAKE RESPONSIBILITY FOR YOUR FUTURE!

This book will show you the lessons that actually work, its proven as I've done it and so have my friends who have followed its lessons, I wanted a better life, it was hard work but I achieved it, now I have had time to look over the good and painful lessons that I originally learnt and really boiled them down to distil them so I had a system that other people can now also follow, so I can arm these people with the information to give them too, the freedom that I now enjoy so much in my life, this freedom is what has allowed me time to be able to write this programme for you to also follow. Now it's not going to be easy but follow the lessons and work your way through them to create a much better life for you and your family.

There is a reason this isn't taught in schools, but it should be...

and

YOU owe it to yourself to be the best version you can be of yourself.

Remember; To get something you never had; you must be ready to do something you never did.

CHAPTER 1

No one gets it easy.

No one gets it easy!

No-one really gets it easy with money, if you're born poor or into a family with very little money, then there are hardships of trying to get yourself out of that situation that you find yourself in, to one of a much better financial position and if your born lucky enough into a family that has money, then this position also has many sets of hurdles and its problems lined up for you, that only people who are in this position can truly understand, either way it's not easy.

But either way I'm sure you know the feeling of working your ass off all day long to earn money only to come home at the end of it tired and drained and also how easy it is to quickly fritter away what you have earnt, if you're not careful and how do you future proof your savings not only from general life but also when you are suddenly hit by a larger event that you didn't know was coming?

For instance, back on 30th January 2020 a virus appeared in China, and it was broadcast on tv around the world as this new virus spread to Italy, then by 11th March 2020, only 2 months later, it had become a full-blown pandemic that the likes of us had never seen and before we could blink, it had spread across the world.
This may all be just a distant memory to you now, or even if you remember it, but governments broadcasted live on tv to their nations to let the population know about a complete shutdown of the country and millions of people had to stay locked in their flats and houses, jobs were at

risk and many small business that had worked so hard for so many years putting in ridiculous hours simply failed, as they had to shut down for such a long time due to government enforcement. Many business's couldn't simply recover from this lack of trading caused and then this made the staff unemployed, no one thought this would ever happen and therefore no one had a plan against such an event, which is why it was a business killer, even the next generation (our children), were severely impacted as they were not allowed to go near or interact with their friends & their education suffered with their mental health, they just couldn't understand why they were not allowed to play with their friends, it was completely unfair.

Let's not mention the nightmare of parents trying to home school, test and mark their children! Let's face it, these awesome parents did their best with what they had.

During this crisis, families also genuinely struggled financially as some employees had to be let go due to reduced numbers of staff needed at places of work to enforce social distancing rules and as mentioned earlier many businesses had to shut down never to reopen again.

In the UK, 39% of the population, about 21 million people, are in financial difficulty and this is mainly due to poor planning for their future.
(Simply put, they spend more than they earn.)

I believe this isn't their fault, as people in general are never given the skills or education required to have a good understanding of money and be able to deal with debt, or able to plan ahead to be able to provide for not only their enjoyment when they are single, but also for planning for their family's future forecast and then into their retirement later on, there is just no financial literacy taught. It's just not explained to us back in school from the grass roots up and because of this I truly believe that the current system of education fails our children to help them toward their future.

They are taught subjects like geography, history and art, but really with this modern world we now live in, they should first be educated with much more important lessons that will set them up for life, subjects like money education to help create a mindset, they should be shown how to manage their personal finances, how to budget and plan for their future, but this doesn't happen because our school system is still outdated and hasn't moved forward quickly enough with our modern times to keep up, some will say that this won't work and the lessons will be boring, well in that case let's make these lessons fun, after all that's what teachers are trained to do, put it this way we all have tried the old school methods of education and please answer this honestly. How did it work out for you or your children, even parents?

I know personally that the lesson I really needed I had to learn the hard way much later on in life and it would of made it so much better if I had friends along the way that were also going through the same things so we could work the issues together, much like you do in a classroom on a problem and this is why a Future Forecast & mindset should be taught at an early age, isn't this why we go to school? So, we can educate ourselves for what is to come and if this subject is such a big one that it effects every day of our adult life then why isn't it taught to you?

Do you see what happens when children are not taught these fundamentals? they will eventually end up with very little or no education on money and then from this point they will then start to develop really bad money management attitudes and habits, think of it this way, children are bought everything they need by their parents, some children can be spoilt but mostly everything they need is simply given to them, they have no ideas truly what the value of an item actually is, if they want it, then it's not normally too long before it appears for them.

Think of it this way, at Christmas or on birthdays have you ever noticed how much children receive in presents now they simply just seem to pile up.

Then from this point how quickly have you seen a children open the wrapping paper look at the gift and then put it to the side right away while they become focused on the next one, they end up with a pile of opened presents where before children were happy to receive that one special gift they longed for and would play with all the time, It's all part of the modern mindset people have now, where things are valued only by the sheer quantity they receive & the speed they can have them, this unrealistic mindset grows further into their late teens, when it expands into being bought the latest video games, top up's or and other high value things and because of this speed of having them (i.e. order now on dads credit card and Amazon will deliver it tomorrow), then the value of these items really don't have an intrinsic value to them.

What I mean by this is that do not appreciate what things cost and it's not their fault as they are being brought up in a society where this is now becoming normal, that is until the day they actually have to go out in the real world and get a job, they then discover very suddenly how little their money actually buys things and life isn't quite so nice as they thought it was, so what do they do?

Well, most get a credit card and get early into debt, why? Because it's made easy to apply for credit and receive one, but this is the start of debt piling up for them and falling into the trap of a very serious debt situation, where most will never escape from its won't be long as the years go by that they will then be at a point where for them they believe it's too late.

Imagine if they had to go back to the times where you had to actually have the money in cash in your pocket and they then had to go to the store and physically hand it over themselves, this old school system would certainly change their attitude to money if they had to work for it to receive cash and then hand it out, it would have more of a meaning of what things costs, it's just made to easy for them to get into debt with cards and mobile devices now.

Children and young adults have no real knowledge on how money works, or how to plan ahead in order to forecast their future, they are taught no personal money skills in school at all, and as mentioned before this is where the trouble starts because when they finally grow older and get to earn money they simply don't have the basic money skills or the knowledge base to be able to look after it, even young people who make a fortune being 'YouTube' stars, sports athletes, or lottery winners, mostly they end up broke in their later years as they don't know how to manage their finances, even if they make it.

In reflecting upon my education, particularly in relation to money matters, I have come to the realization that the information provided to children in schools is quite limited. It is common for us to believe that teachers are equipping us with knowledge that will be valuable throughout our lives, and as a young student, I placed my trust in them.

The conventional path laid out for me was to attend school, followed by college, achieve good grades, and then proceed to university to secure a great job. However, as I navigate through life now, I find that the majority of the knowledge I rely upon daily is rooted in the foundational principles I learned during my early years. Allow me to elaborate on this point.

In kindergarten we begin to learn to interact and make friends with people we don't know, then maths is taught in the form of the basic arithmetic, adding, subtraction, multiplication, and division, and of course your primary spoken language.

We learn to write and develop these skills and get better as time goes by, but do you notice that many of the most important tasks that you do every day even right now as you read this, consist of use basic skills for example, Maths when you're buying or selling things or paying bills so you know how much money you have in your pocket, your spoken language...so you can communicate effectively and your writing skills.

Then as you progress past school you are urged that to be able to get a better job in life, you need to go to college and then university, from here you are taught more complex maths or skills, but if you have taken this route to university, let me ask you this....Do you still use the skills and topics that you were taught from college or university in your job right now in our modern world?

For example: If you're an engineer years ago you used to spend hour after hour memorising equations, but now they don't need to do this as this information is available online and accessible easily with a simple mobile phone.

Do you really have to remember all the equations you were taught years ago? chances are that when you need to recall data from the past that you would of more than likely forgotten what the equation was anyway, and it would need looking up!

But I bet you do use basic arithmetic more in your everyday life, in order pay bills or buy things you need! Maybe you use the basic arithmetic to work out how long it will take to pay back your student loans or debts that you accumulated!

We really do need to be given a more rounded education and it's never too late, but it would be easier to do this obviously at a young age, don't you think that after you are taught the basics of education (basic maths, English, science etc..) then it would of been good for you to get better at them and then also be taught through play and interaction about the basic skills to explain how money works, to have the skills to know what an asset or a liability is and to know good debt from bad debt, learn how banks make money from you when you deposit it and how generally the money system works so the school can give you a fighting chance, maybe let pupils start up at school a small class based business that they can learn how to run one though fun and role play, (my daughter opened a small business selling fidget spinners off her own merit and the school stopped her doing this, they would rather try to kill her sprit for wanting to try something that will provide feedback to her about starting a small business and benefit her in life, than actually praise her and encouraging a new up and coming person with an entrepreneurial spirit.

So why did they stop her? Rather than praise her and offer advice and encouragement?), it's because teachers don't have a clue about money either, as it wasn't taught to them in school when they were young and they don't understand the system either, They also live in fear that they can't write anything like this book or speak up and teach these things or encourage and offer help to young people who are trying to start up their own bit of small business because if they do, they will be at risk of losing their job and if that happens then they can't afford to pay their own bills.

How bad is this, our children are being taught life lessons by people who weren't given these skills either, have got in debt and need their jobs just to pay the bills, but they are now in a position where they can't make changes and don't because they are in fear of losing their jobs and income!

I intend to start to correct this right now for everyone who reads on!

We are going to work and move forward together, I am going to supply you with information that you should of been taught at an early age to help you with your personal finances & planning that will allow you to grow and prosper, it's not too late to learn this for yourself and also pass this to other people you know young and old in order to help them too.

This book has been designed to solely provide you to be able to create your future in the form of a large target to aim for, the methods and lesson will change the way you think about money for ever, it will also allow you to plan ahead for your future, so you can have peace of mind knowing that you have old age covered, all while you are enjoying life a little more doing the things you really want to do while you are young enough to be able to in the meantime.

So let me ask you.

- Do you have any assets?

- Do you have a flat or a house?

- Do you have any other properties, a bank account, or any savings?

- Where is your money coming from & what does this all mean for your future?

And the big question:

What if you decided right now

TO STOP WORKING

or

You became I'll & Life made the decision to stop for you?

Let me ask you, could you happily walk off into the sun and do everything you always wanted to do without the fear that you won't run out of money when you reach old age?

We've all seen older people working at hardware stores, depots, van driving high street shops, you've more than likely seen them working at fast food chains.

But why are they there?
Is it because these people miss the fun of working?
Or is it because they are running out of funds in their later years and they need to earn as much money as they can, to be able to live and now it's a rush to earn that while they are still physically able to work.

Did they spend too much money in their past buying things they couldn't afford & they now have to pay the price for this in their old age, when they should be enjoying life,

Do you want this for your Future?

Or perhaps you belong to the group of individuals who have successfully accumulated a modest sum of extra money over time, yet find themselves unable to retire and enjoy the fruits of their labour. Despite having earned the opportunity to relax and indulge in life's pleasures, you persist in working tirelessly. It begs the question: why do you continue to toil endlessly, burdened by the sense of obligation to pay your bills?

So, when old age finally arrives, YES you do have a lot of money in the bank, but now you don't have the youth or strength to do the things you always wanted to do.
All those dreams you had of adventure & travel that you always spoke about to your friends, saying:

"When I've retired, I'm going to........."

But now you're old and physically limited and you can't do what you used to be able to, which may not be what you envisioned you would be like when you thought about the long distant subject of old age when you were much younger.

What happens when you get old, and you end up having some health issues that require you to now need some sort of medical help or care?

I'm not sure if you're aware but the government will not provide it for you at the moment of writing this book if you have money saved up and many years later from me writing this, I'm sure it will be worse for the population. Please pay attention here because the dream we were all sold which was, work hard all your life then when your older all that tax you paid into a pot will be there so you can retire and enjoy yourself and you will be looked after in your golden years, this was a complete lie sold to you all, and we were all stupid enough to believe it,

The truth is you worked like a slave all your life, you have paid your taxes and now you've retired(do you know that over the average working life you paid nearly 55% of all your income in some form of tax to the government?) that's over half of all your money, then add in inflation and stealth taxes and on average your lucky to keep around 30 to 40% of what you earn.

They say that buying a home is your biggest debt, well that's simply not true, your biggest debt is actually the government that you work for.

Have you noticed that after a long week or month of work you look at your pay packet and the government takes it taxes off you first, before you even receive your payslip, you haven't even received your money yet and the government knows that you don't have a way to forecast your financial future and they don't trust you to pay them, therefore they take it off you at source before it is even paid to you.

So now you have worked all your life and you're at an age where you must stop working,

'Welcome To Your Retirement Age!' (or whatever age it is now as the government keeps moving the goal posts on this one!) congratulations you're now an official drain on the system, because you're not paying into it any more, if you have any funds saved away in the bank then this will be used by the government first to pay for any health care you need, they will even sell your home if your cash runs out and you still need care, at the time of writing this when your money drops down to the 'total sum' of all your assets (cash and property) is less than £14,000 only then will the government help, but they will only supply you with the BASIC amount to keep you going, you won't be in a lavish lifestyle, so be warned well in advance here!

If you didn't enjoy your money when you were young and just worked all the time, then you will now watch it very quickly dwindle away in old age, you may as well spend all the cash, sold the house and blown that on a good time then entered retirement with less than 14,000 to your name.

Why did I say that, well simply because if you die leaving something then the government will swoop in to be first in line, they will claim their massive death taxes and the solicitors will be employed to do this for them on their behalf and your personal estate, or what's left of it, will pick up their bill for this before whatever is left gets passed down to your loved ones.

How nice of you to spend your entire life working for everyone else, paying your taxes when you had to and now your dead!

Whatever money you have left over will be charged as inheritance tax, so if you wanted to pass any money or property you had left over down to loved ones to help them get a foot on the ladder then this has its own set of problems now, that you have unknowingly left for them to pay for and sort out and if you die alone with no family to pass anything down to, then all that remains will go directly to the state or your government automatically.

Whatever path you may take the fact is, your money is going to get taken from you and why?

Well, it's all because you didn't enjoy it first!

You didn't spend it or give it away to a cause or anyone that YOU chose too early on when you had the power to do so, and because of your failure to act on or plan for this in advance, it will now get spent...for you,

'If only you had a way of planning ahead to avoid this problem!'

In this book, you will learn ways to use the information provided to plan for your future to have financial control over your life. I want you to work through the processes that I will teach you, so you can see what your (£ or $) amount you will need to be able to enjoy your life now.

So, what is the amount that you need to enable you to do the things you love.

How much do you really need for YOUR perfect life?

Is it 100,000? 500,000? 1,000,000?

Or more?

I don't want you to spend the rest of your life working away in a forever repeating cycle and not enjoying yourself, forget subjects at school that teach you nothing about the real world, the teachers should be arming you with tools like how money works and budgets and how debt works so you can create the building blocks for your future.

'It's not rocket science!'

You can do many more physical things in your 40s and 50s than in your 80s & 90s…..... so the quicker you understand the method that I will show you, the quicker you can improve the quality of life for yourself and your loved ones and start living a good life now in the most important years of our short lives.

There is also no point saving your money till the end of your days, working every hour and just hoarding it and never spending any of it to enjoy life as you want it all for when you retire, all that will happen is that you will end up spiteful and eventually die wealthy then the tax man will get most of it, so remember you can't take it with you!

This book will show you that you can earn it, spend it and leave as little as possible when we are older and we can plan that NOW.

Let me put it this way.

Have you ever seen a removal van following behind a hearse carrying all of the dead person's possessions?

NO?

Do you know why?

Because if you go back in history you will find that the Egyptians tried it first…they believed that when they died they should be buried and all of their possessions should be taken with them for the afterlife…..

Do you know ultimately what happened to them?

'They Just Got Robbed Anyway'

Now when you read this book, let me give you a warning, the grammar isn't going to be the best and if you read a lot of books then you may think it's terrible and there might even be spelling mistakes, but just so you know...

I don't care.

so please don't waste your time writing to me to tell me about any mistakes you found.

I'm not creating a work of English literature to last forever. I'm not JK Rowling; I'm just trying to create a book to help you get off the rat run and go enjoy yourself while you are able to, so if you spend more time picking this book apart then this says more about you than me.

It's sole purpose is to provide education & help you enjoy life now and plan for the future so you can get out of the rat race and enjoy your life to do the things you love before you get too old and end up sat in a chair all day soiling your nappy in front of a tv, wishing you did that thing you always wanted to do, but you never took the time off to just go do it.

I have created this book and the information it contains only for the reader (YOU) and you alone.

I want to give you the tools to understand the basic skills of a Future Forecaster that I use every day, so I can adjust my plan whenever I want so I can make sure I allow myself time to enjoy the things I want to do, while I can.

If I hit a crossroad then the data can be adjusted so I can see the repercussions that that issue may cause in advance and then I readjust, so it does not affect me later down the line.

These skills of money management and planning should be taught to all children in schools, so they can also enjoy life having fun and be able to plan for their future many years in advance.... but for some reason....it isn't.

Children get their education from teachers who most have never run a business or managed money in any way, they struggle and are most likely skint (otherwise they would shake the education tree, but they can't afford to, just in case they lose their job). So, these are the people that are chosen to best educate our children and to train their minds for the real world, children are on the back foot to start with and most only start to understand about it when it's too late, for example when they end up in some form of debt.

The government and education system decides that teaching money management and how it works just isn't in

YOUR BEST INTEREST,

after all, if you work hard and pay taxes then you stay poor for your whole life with no chance of escape, so you must work week after week to repeat the cycle.

So if children are not going to be educated with a money mindset then I would like to help as many people as I can get a better financial knowledge, I feel it's my mission to provide this information to you, it's something I was taught by my mentors and it has massively changed my life, my only regret is that I wish I was taught it earlier as I would have had a lot more experiences under my belt, but learning this has changed my life and now I want to offer a hand out to help you, so you can use the information you already have to show what is possible for your future and truly make it happen for you. We are going to take the position you are in now and plot your destination, the inbetween bit is what we need to do to get there .

Wealth isn't about who has the most money.

It's about you having enough that it will give you **OPTIONS** & choices you did not have before!

You can also help other people a lot more when you know you are financially stable.

CHAPTER 2

My Story

My Story…

This book isn't a poor sob story you so often hear on TV.

This story is I'm sorry to say…is true & even though I understand it's an extreme example! Nonetheless, it happened to me & because it did, it could also just as easily happen to you, so if only one person in 100000 listens and takes in this example and uses it to their advantage, then to me, it's been worth the time of typing it and reliving the pain once again by me putting this matter onto paper.

Just so you know I have never done this before until today, so it's going to be therapy for me too, I will say that I'm not looking forward to it, but here we go for the both of us but it's mainly for your benefit and if it changes the way you plan for your future to help you create a way forward with your family, then it was 100% worth it!

There is a though a purpose to this story, a lesson, if you will…. so here I go.

My parents met when they were 16 and spent all their time hanging out with each other as most young couples do. They got married as soon as they could. My mum then was a photographer, and my dad became a welder. When they were 25, they decided to start their own welding business, all they could afford at that time was a small place to start from, and a family business began. It was situated in an old coal shed with a toilet. It was back in 1968, and the toilet was a bucket! (I am not joking, that is what we have!)

They lived in a caravan until they had enough money saved up to be able to afford to move into a small converted flat. As the years went by, my parents had earnt enough money from hard work to rent their 1st decent small commercial unit with an actual working toilet & later on, in 1974 I was born.

Like most children my age in the 70's, I never saw my dad growing up. This is not a moan or poor me; it's just how it was. My dad was always working! As he had to, sometimes he would come home at 5pm to grab some food and see us, and then he would sleep in the chair for about an hour and go straight back to work and be there all night, then we wouldn't see him till about 6 am the next day, he did this for 3 or 4 days at a time, before going back to average 12- or 13-hours days. When he wasn't so busy, he always worked, trying his hardest to get any job in the business so he could pay bills.

School events & sports days used to come and go, and my dad was never there. Arguments between my mum and dad took place a lot.

My mum used to tell him he was not the carefree man he was when they first met, but they always patched it up as they were a team, but it was the work that supplied the stress for them both.

I only found out 40 years later that the reason for all this was my dad wanted to come to my events but at that time, he had two mortgages, one for the home and another for the business, and he could not spend the time to come and see me at my events as every waking hour was needed to earn money, so he could pay the bills and keep my mum and I fed and clothed and buy stock for the business. It wasn't an easy time, as you could imagine, if he missed a day working if was us that suffered.

Don't get me wrong, my dad wasn't a bad one, far from it. He was a fantastic, loving man back who spent any remaining time he had with us. He didn't go to the pub like most men if he could. He would only be in 2 places, one was at work and when he wasn't working, he'd be at home in some form with us when he could, but I mainly saw him when I used to get up and go with my father to the business at 6:30am on a Saturday. I did this only so I could spend more time with him, even if it meant sitting in a lorry while delivering what he had produced the week before, or just sat in meeting while he talked to contactors, at the time I didn't realise that by doing this I was passively learning too.

Now back in the 1970's if you had a holiday, no one went abroad the best you could hope for was a week in a caravan. My friends couldn't believe it we were going to another country on a plane. It just didn't happen to ordinary people back then! But once a year, my dad would find the time and somehow find the money for us to go to Spain (you might not appreciate this, but back in 70's this was like being a rock star!)

When we were there, I had ALL his time. We went to water parks, where we would go on the slides and act like a couple of kids for days. We ate ice cream till we felt sick, had milkshakes and basically anything that now would be classed as bad for you, we went snorkelling on the beach, and we made so many happy memories, just my mum, my dad and I acted like children as we were all young at heart, it was magical to spend this time as a family, but when it was over & we got back home to the UK, that was it and I was lucky to see him when I could again as he had to return to work for us.

I remember many arguments between my mum and dad as the business seemed to take control and consume everything we did, it controlled our lives and the ability to just have time together and it its grip tightened as the business grew, as inevitably all small businesses seem to do.

We needed employees to help us take off the strain, but this created a new problem as they seemed to need babysitting for most of the tasks we required from them, every aspect of the business seemed to take over everything we did, and I thought my parents would split up through their ever-growing arguments and stress it created.

Everyone used to call my dad a workaholic, and he used to reply with, "As soon as I've got enough money, that's it, I'm out of here, we'll retire to Spain, and I'll buy a house and enjoy my life, mark my words." but people used to laugh at him as they knew it wouldn't happen, my dad would work till he dropped.

Many years later, my mum and dad had finally achieved the goal or the destination they were working so hard toward, they could finally now retire now they were both around the age of 65 years old. They had put in years of hard slog & sacrificed a lot to get to this point, so much more than most people could even begin to imagine, and then he broke the news to everyone's disbelief.

"That's it!" he said. "We've bought a place in Spain, your mum & I are off to live the good life. We've earnt the right to live in Spain in the winter and the UK in the summer. I told you I'm not a workaholic. It just took me 50 years to get where I wanted." To our amazement, that's what he did, he retired, true to his word.

Mum and dad really enjoyed this new life. They experienced Spain during the day with the clean beaches and the restaurants at night. My mum said that shortly after they both moved there, that the miserable businessman who had grown in the form of my father suddenly died, and he was replaced by the man that she remembered all those years ago when they were both young.

He was carefree at last and they both were enjoying the life they craved out together.

Six months later on a bright sunny day my parents were driving back to their villa after going to the supermarket, they were on a dead straight road on a warm clear day a car was passing them the other way, and at the last second it swerved crossing the lane and collided with them at speed.

The driver of the car was intoxicated (Drunk) and if he was driving his car half a second earlier or even later he would have completely missed them, but that didn't happen; it was fate and my mum died in the sudden impact, my dad managed to survive the crash with terrible injuries and spent months in hospital healing, when he was finally strong enough to make the journey home to the UK, he lived with the guilt that they both worked so hard for their entire lives, never taking time to enjoy it and then it was over, before they got a chance to enjoy what they had worked so hard for!

My dad said, "Why didn't we enjoy it earlier and do what your mum wanted to do?"

My mum always wanted to go to New York or on a Cruise, but they decided to wait until the golden years which sadly never came for them.

My dad also died about 4 years later from a broken heart, he struggled with the fact they had both worked for the day they could enjoy life and it never happened, he found it hard to keep going every day without the one person in his life he truly adored (some people say this is a myth, but I can vouch that this is true & tragically, it does happen, especially when you lose someone who is the sole reason for your existence).

So, they were both dead (you probably think that I got to inherit everything, well no I did not, because we never talked about future planning we found it too morbid, we always said we would do it later, but we never did), and our reward for this was that any money they had worked so hard for....they never got to spend for themselves to enjoy.

Next was the tax man, who appeared very quickly and demanded his pound of flesh. He went through everything they had and then the massive taxes were charged.

The main thing of value was the business and they demanded that if I didn't pay the tax, the business would be sold and that would be the end of that, but one way or another they would be paid their taxes.

Anything my parents had built up over the years was gone by the time the government had finished. Even my parents dream home in Spain, which was just a modest 3-bedroom place (nothing fancy), had to be sold to pay solicitor fees and medical expenses, (the UK tax man also checks what you have abroad). Hence, you pay UK inheritance tax, Spanish tax & the local town's taxes and fees.

I know this sounds morbid, so why am I telling you this? (well this is just a fraction of the story, as it got much worst for us in Spain, but that's something different).

So what's the point of this story?
Simple, I don't want the same to happen to you or your family. Yes work hard, but with the correct planning of your money, you can enjoy your time, spend your money when it matters, go on that cruise or holiday to New York or what you want and buy the things you always wanted don't wait…

LIVE YOUR LIFE…

NOW!

It's crucial about planning what you have, what you are earning, and how you spend, invest, and save it.

The aim of the 'Game of life' is to enjoy what you have, do the things you want to do and buy the things you want then somewhere near the end of your life, leave just enough to bury you with.

The perfect example if you follow the 'Future Forecast' lessons in this book to build up what you have, assets, cash, savings accounts, etc. Then you can see at what age you have the most funds and go spend it, just enjoy those years while you can, travel the world, treat yourself or give it to family in the form of treating them when you can and enjoy your hard work. You fucking earned it, after all!

Then the skill is that if you plan towards what age you believe you will live to, then you can design your future and in the best possible scenario at the exact moment of your death, it's the single digit to the tax man and his mob and you leave this world with just enough money in your name to hand over the last little bit of top up money to your loved ones, small enough that they don't pay tax on it and what's left over is only enough to bury you with. The tax man gets nothing.

That's the plan, the game, and the target to aim at!

This book has been created to do one thing, helping you to protect yourself and understand how money works well enough in advance of your later years, that you can make intelligent decisions in advance of this to benefit yourself and those you care about.

Now there is not a totally correct or perfect number value for how much money you will need for your retirement fund, everyone is different, but I want you to understand the power you have and your course for where you are heading right now, lets change the course and direction of your life massively just by altering your system of how you plan for the future by knowing where you are right now and the desired destination you are headed for, this will arm you with great peace of mind to plot that course and not just live life floating about with no purpose or direction.

Let's make you the captain of your own ship, it's your job to plot a course, set your direction and go for it!

If you don't enjoy your money
& spend it when you're breathing…

THEN

**The Taxman will do it for you
when you're not.**

CHAPTER 3

What's Your Magic Number?

What's Your Magic Number?

Without being silly and just pulling a high number out of thin air for example, "I want 10 million!"

The question is, how much do you need to enjoy your life?

Do you worry that at the moment you may not have the funds to be able to enjoy life in the future?

If you're reading this book, then the chances are that it is a concern to you and you must think about this matter at multiple points over the years, "Have I got enough money?" and do you want to end up not spending anything in the good years when you should be having fun?

When do you wish to retire?

45?

50?

60+

Do you know when you will be able to afford to do this?

Do you want to be still working late in life, tired, resentful, and stressed instead of enjoying yourself?

Would you like to be working at a burger restaurant in your golden years only because you must?

And if you spend money on something big for yourself now, then are you concerned about what happens when that exciting buzz you initially had wears off, like buying a sports car or going on a big holiday?

Then somehow, it's now got to be paid for afterwards. Do you know? If you can you even afford it long-term?

Putting yourself in a box is no way to live your life. You need to enjoy precious moments with your family and loved ones. What do you want to do? Is it to travel the globe, have great holidays and build memories?

Do you want to do this before your body gets too old and physically cannot allow you to do the things you always want to?

So, don't let these opportunities pass you by. You will be able to see them all laid out in front of you so you can tailor your plan to your future.
In this book, I will take you through the process so you can tweak your finances & your Future Forecast mindset.

It will then give you the information to decide if you have enough money right now to start living as you should or if you need to do something about it to increase your funds or cut things out that is bad for you.

Time is the one commodity that even the rich can't buy, sell, or make more of. It's a set length and the trouble is that you don't know when it will end, but one thing's certain, you cannot create any more of it for yourself.

No one ever laid on their deathbed thinking, "I wish I spent more time working."

They usually think, "I wish I spent more time with the kids, went on holiday, travelled more, swam with dolphins, or something else.

But no-one ever looks back wishing they spent more time working.

It's not a matter of if you should plan for your future.

IT'S WHEN!

And if you don't plan now...

Then life will do it for you the hard way!

CHAPTER 4

Why Me?

Why Me?

Now you're probably thinking, why is he the best person to cover this subject? Well, when it comes to most things, then I consider myself a bit of an expert in being able to listen to what is said, then soak it all up and then reiterate it in a way to keep things simple, buzz words and technical wording complicates things, keep it simple and everyone understands it a little better.

Yes, you can use finical advisors; and if you have one, that's fantastic, but many people don't have one, don't know where to start and don't know how to plan for their future as it was never taught to them, so I want to give you something to help with that.

This book aims to give you a bit of primary education, removing all the buzzwords that financial advisors use and keeping it simple, because with just a little education, which is what I am going to give you, then the best advisor to advise and plan for your future isn't someone else.
IT'S YOU!

You are the captain of your own ship and you're going to set its own course for a destination that YOU will choose. My lessons contained here will help show up any pitfalls before they happen, so you can navigate around them in plenty of time to avoid them or and then set your course straight again well before they happen, consider this much like a ship's radar.

A Little About Me

I was also one of these people who worked daily; I earned
my weekly wages, got paid on a Thursday, spent it by
Sunday, and then for some reason I repeated the weekly
cycle always looking forward to Friday for some reason.
When wages were then changed to be paid on a monthly
cycle then I felt so rich on pay day but toward the end of
the month you seemed to be living poor!
On and on it went. I worked from the age of 16 and I also
juggled my college and University life working too, when
my friends had the summer off as they got student grants, I
must spend my holidays working to be able to earn enough
money to look pay my rent and food when I returned back
at education.

I came from a family of hard-working people you see, and
I wasn't taught about any form of saving or education in
money management but one day I just had enough of the
constantly repeating cycle and one day the first piece of
advice was given to me by someone I trusted very much, I
was introduced to the method of splitting up my wages and
putting it into jars as we were paid in cash back, but years
on I find that some banks now allow you to do this
digitally at the time of writing this.

I had one jar for my rent, one for my gas supply, one for
electricity, a spare one for any change I had left over from
going to buy things & one for food. I would work out what
I needed for every month and then put a portion into each
jar, so at the end of the month, even though I might of

spent all my money, I knew I had the right amount in each jar to cover all my essential bills and that they would be paid.

I could keep a roof over my head, if I had any loose change, I would put this into the odd change jar, and it would slowly build up over time with any loose change I had, when it was full I would empty it and count up what I had, I then took the contents of the jar to the bank so I could get it changed into notes and from there I would either use it to buy something I really needed or I would put it into a saving account, so it was always slowly being topped up, this way I could invest this money into something that would help me in the future.

You see when my parents died, I saw what happened to the pot of money they had worked so hard and sacrificed so many things for to be able to enjoy retirement, they left it too late to enjoy it and then it just all got taken away.

It changed my opinion of the image of everyday people who work so hard all their life in the hope of enjoying it in the future, that wasn't for me, I want to enjoy it now!

So, I continued to use my savings to educate myself when I could.

I have spent a small fortune on mentors and self-education and continue to do so today. I have learned new creative ways of making money, how to multiply it and how money actually works.

Why am I constantly educating myself still, as you now know I was made an orphan in my early 30's and very suddenly on both occasions, where my parents were talking to me one day as healthy as you are now and only a few hours later my amazing parents who care for me so much and were the most important things to me in the world were gone forever and I vowed this would not be my future too, by 36, I started the new journey of my education, and by 45, I was financially free! (This term is something you may of heard of before, but if you haven't then what it really means is this; that passive money that you earn, i.e. inflows of money that you don't work for like rent from properties, interest on savings etc. is the same amount as all your debts like gas electric rent etc. effectively stating that if you now stopped working right now, you can survive quite happily for the rest of your life.)

I'm not bragging, far from it, I'm just letting you know that even though it's not easy, **I did it!** I created a new money mindset and if one person can do it then why can't 2, 3 or more people also follow and do it for themselves too.

Your probably thinking, it's okay for him, I've got this or that, it's too hard to do, but guess what?
Lots of things worth doing aren't easy; it just takes commitment, discipline, time, and sacrifice, all that separates you and me is a little education that I'm going to give you now, so the only thing it will come down to is whether you decide to act on this information to better your life.

In my youth when my friends went out every weekend drinking and having fun, I was the one pushing my limits educating and growing myself. I gave up quite a bit in search of my goal.

However, I can now enjoy my life free from most hassles where my old friends are still in the same never-ending cycle, just like times haven't changed for them.
They still don't have any money and still moan about having no money when they go out, but they are unwilling to change. When I don't see them for a period of time and then meet up its quite shocking how far forward, I have travelled where they are still static, even now I'm still attending courses and travelling to meet new people where I can ask questions and learn from them and then return the favour.

Again, I'm not trying to brag in any way. I just want to imprint on you again that even me (who wasn't very good at keeping money in my pocket at first), could learn to quickly change my future with just a little help and a bit of information.

I was learning and creating a new system as I went along, making mistakes as I went along and if it took me ten years to get out of the position I was in to where I am now, then you should be able to do this in less time as the system has already been created and tested.

I have already done all the hard work for you, and now I'm going to be supplying the information for you to use, so you now have a head start on me from when I started.

In this book, I'm putting my knowledge into the melting pot and really boiling it down so I can give you the good distilled stuff, life slips away pretty quickly and it seems to speed up as you get older, so let's get that life you want and you go and do the things you want to do, before old age creeps up on you, because if you wait till this moment to do anything then it's too late.

I now also spend a lot of time consulting with small businesses and individual's who want to start businesses to help them achieve their goals. If you are wondering why I only choose small businesses, this is because that is where I also started and I found it very lonely back then and you felt entirely on my own, as I had no-one to discuss running a business with.

If I had help back then, I could have been a lot better off and wouldn't of made as many mistakes as I did and lost so much time, so I now offer my services to small businesses with their problems and pain points, believe me you are not alone, if you have any issues or question or just need to discuss ideas then reach out to my team or me, and we will be here for you.

CHAPTER 5

Educating Ourselves

Educating Ourselves

Now I want to help as many people as possible to gain a better understanding of financial knowledge and help them move forward with their direction in life, as the subject of money is never taught to us when we are young, we are just left to figure it out by ourselves as I have mentioned earlier.

Maybe your parents gave you some life skills and taught you about money, or maybe you were not so lucky.

I mention this because the world has changed massively since your parents' youth. They were most likely taught to work hard every day and work long hours and save money, if they did then you may have heard them tell you about these quotes before:

"A penny saved is a penny earned."

"Look after the pennies, and the pounds will follow."

"Money doesn't grow on trees, you know."

"I'm not made of money."

They did this because, in the old days, saving your money had some value, but banks who print obscene amounts of new money every day using quantitative easing (this is what is meant by the government printing money when they need it, but this devalues the value of what things cost)and it ends up debasing or devalues what your money can buy and therefore what it is worth.

They pay you nothing in interest, yet they loan your money to others at around 30% and make a fortune. Think of it this way, you are led to believe that putting your money in a bank is safe, yet the bank does not even guarantee your money is safe, normally the FCA do this instead.

You now need to clear your head of all the old phrases that were drilled into you as we covered above and create new ones that are more relative to today's money world.

Look let's put it quite simply…

"If you're worried about stopping to pick up a penny, then you'll miss the pounds, euros or dollars floating by".

With high inflation, money is worth less every day if you just put it in the bank and it erodes what you can actually buy with it. Take for example for easy figures if you have 10% inflation, this means that if you have £1000 in your bank and you leave it there, then a year later its worth 10% less, so what you could buy a year before for £1000 will actually cost 10% more for £1100.

This information would be so helpful to our children as they grow up to help keep them out of debt, but there just not taught the basics of money management in school.

Our children are being taught life lessons by their teachers and tutors who most likely are broke too, as they themselves also never received any financial education, when they were younger of how they could manage themselves about money or how money works in the real world and if they try to teach this subject in school to help students, then they are stopped from doing so and may lose their jobs, this fear keeps the teachers in check too.

They teach our children subjects like business studies, yet these teachers must work every day until retirement, in their job.

As mentioned earlier on if they lose their job as a teacher, they are financially fucked! So, what chance do your children have in the future learning off them?
Wouldn't it be better to learn off someone who has achieved their goal and is still pushing hard forward, rather than someone who teaches a 45-minute lesson then sit's in the staff canteen waiting for Friday or payday to arrive?

I want to give every person the chance to read this book and go through the steps to gain some primary financial education and knowledge that you can implement immediately to your life right now and even pass the lessons down to your children as life seems to pass so quickly these days.

Have you ever booked a holiday and it seems to take forever for it to arrive?

Next thing you know, it's here, and you've got a week or two off work.

Whooooo.....hooooo !!!!

Just a couple of days in, and you're loving it, and you've got all this time off, its great!
Next thing you know, you are home and then back to work, and the holiday was two weeks ago...
What the hell happened?

This is the same with age. One minute we are at school playing with our friends, and the next, we are adults with jobs and maybe even children and the bills to prove it.

Look, we are all eventually headed for the same place, but this book is all about how the journey will be for you along the way.

I enjoy my life and I also want that for you too and this book will help you.

I'm a great believer that something special happens to us at some point in life every now and then, what you must do is recognise it when it happens and then act upon it before the opportunity leaves.

Remember:

If you always do what you have always done…

Then you will ALWAYS get what you always got!

So, let's get started, shall we?

CHAPTER 6

Your Money

Earlier on, I mentioned how I learnt about a method of applying my wages into different jars and putting money aside to cover my costs of living when I was younger, this is a system that has developed over the years and still works well for me.

I have now taken my original method and have evolved it to something quite different now in order to move with the times, I will explain to you the workings and their basic processes now.

Imagine, if you will, that you have a large jar/cup/bucket or whatever you find easier to imagine. In my case, I will be using a plastic bucket as we may have to drill some holes in this later (don't worry just follow along, I haven't lost my mind!).

The purpose of this bucket is to hold all the money you currently have, but please be aware that it can only hold money that you currently have or is readily available, for instance, money in your pocket, any change, or a considerable amount of cash! Maybe you have money stashed away in a bank account or savings account. Do you have an ISA or any form of stock? Or just a excess of money after you get paid.

We are talking about any form of cash that you can get your hands on very quickly, the sort of stuff you could spend easily if you wanted, BUT NO CREDIT CARDS are allowed here please!

This section is all about **readily available cash.**

Now visualise that with a wave of a magic wand your money magically turned into a liquid. It can be any liquid you wish: water, milk, wine, soft drinks, anything!

But visualise your cash turning into a liquid, and now you will pour it into your bucket to see how much it fills up.

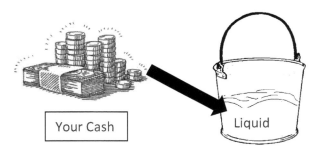

The next thing to think about is, do you have any property?

Most people think of the home they are living in as an asset, but is it?
You may have your own home, or you may have inherited one from someone else in the past, but let me explain what an asset is:

An asset is something that puts money in your pocket, whereas a liability is something that takes money out of your pocket!

So, if you have a rental property then the cash flow you get from this property, for example, the money you get from the rent minus mortgage payment, expenses, etc. is an asset and this money you should turn into liquid and put into your bucket.

So, your own home is a liability, I know you think it's an asset, as you have probably been told this by numerous people over the years, but let me ask you this:

In your home at the moment, do you pay a mortgage? Things like bills, expenses, council tax, etc.

Yes, you do!

And does this house generate any cash flow for you regularly? Or does it give you any free cash every month?

No?

Then your home is, I'm afraid, a liability!

Yes, I do understand that your house is worth more now than you originally paid for it, but this extra money is stuck in the house and tied up until you finally sell it in order to release it and this could take months in order to free it up and until you do that, you can't spend the cash.

Take for instance if you needed to buy food to feed your family, you simply can't remove a wall in your home and sell it to get the cash to buy food, it's a long-drawn-out process and not therefore liquid at the moment.

So, your home and your cash you keep separate as shown below.

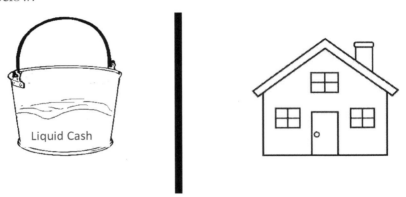

Now, if in the future you ever decide to re-mortgage your house to pull out the equity from it, that's the difference between what you bought it for and what it's worth now, or maybe you decide just to sell your home, as maybe you just don't need a place that is so big now (maybe the kids have moved out!)

So, you can now buy a new home that's not so big, some call this downsizing.

The difference in value is that you sell the old house for and the cost of buying the new smaller one then that becomes liquid cash that you can spend if you wish, so you must imagine this is now liquid.

You can now pour this liquid cash into your bucket along with what's already there to increase the volume you have in the bucket; this could help you greatly in the future and top up any money you have spent in the past while you were spending your money enjoying yourself.

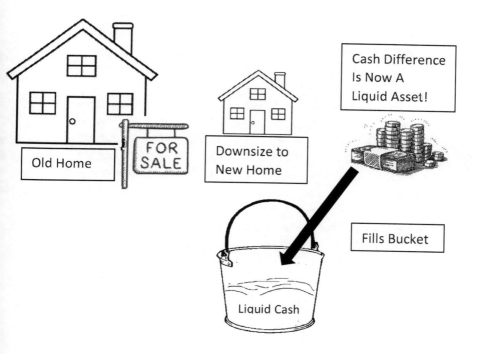

Old Home

FOR SALE

Downsize to New Home

Cash Difference Is Now A Liquid Asset!

Fills Bucket

Liquid Cash

The next big thing is a pension, if you have one, I'm afraid this is yet another liability as you are forever putting money from your wages into it. While you don't see any rewards or benefits and you cannot use it or get any cash out, when it's in the pension pot, it's just another outgoing cost from your money that gets locked into a safe (called a pension pot) and you can't open it until you reach a certain age.

Cash Outgoing

Pension Pot

Now, for example, in the UK, you can start drawing an income from a private pension after the age of 55 if you wish. This means that after 55 years old, rather than the income you earn getting sent to the pension pot that is locked away from you with no access, you can now start to draw it back to you. It will drip monthly into your current account to act as an income. This then becomes a liquid asset (as you can spend it), now this is the time you can add this drip to your bucket as the level within it will increase over time if you don't spend it, much like putting a bucket under a leak from a dripping ceiling.

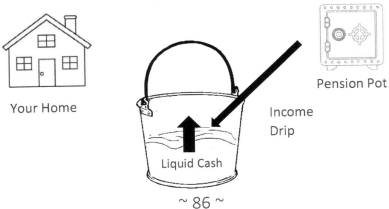

Your Home

Pension Pot

Income Drip

Liquid Cash

Suppose you are a business owner or have a second home. In this case, you will need to allow it to be kept separate & away from your bucket (as again, "it is a liability.") due to the fact you can't get out any large amounts of cash out unless you sell them like before.

So, it has no actual cash value until the day you decide to sell it. After you have sold it, the money you receive after the tax becomes a liquid asset, as it can then be spent.

| Your Home | Pension Pot | A Business or 2nd Home you own. |

Your money is tied up OUTSIDE YOUR LIQUID CASH BUCKET.

INSIDE your bucket

Money in Liquid Form
(Easily Available)

CHAPTER 7

Money That Comes In.

Money that comes in.

Now we will look at money that currently flows into your bucket. Take, for example, that you are currently still working. This means you have a regular income/wage paid into your bank account each week or month, which would be your main income flow.

Do you have a 2nd job or get dividends from a business you own? If you have a second home you rent out; this will also be another liquid income while you receive it. You can also include any benefits you receive.

We call this a secondary income flow.

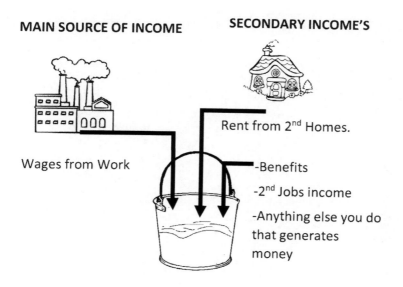

MAIN SOURCE OF INCOME   **SECONDARY INCOME'S**

Rent from 2nd Homes.

Wages from Work

-Benefits

-2nd Jobs income

-Anything else you do that generates money

Now the income currently flowing into your bucket right now is based on the fact of your current situation.
When you get older and you decide to retire, your wages will stop, or when the children get to a certain age, the child benefits will stop, so your income is time dependent.

Let's say you owned a shop or small business from which you take a wage, and one day at the age of 55, you may decide to sell it or just shut it down. The day this happens, then the income it gave you will stop (for example, it gave you weekly wages until you are 55 years old, and then this regular income will no longer exist from that point onward) so at that moment at the same time, this money is transient (meaning its always moving hopefully toward your bucket).

It will eventually end.
Then as with everything else in life, something else will take its place.

For example, as mentioned above, you shut the business down at 55, and your wages stop. Still, you could start to draw down from the private pension that you or your employer set up, so while the wages have stopped as your primary income at 55, this will be replaced with your regular pension payments.

You may also decide to sell your home (as the children have now moved away and it's now just the 2 of you in a house that's now too big for you both) so you downsize to a smaller one. Or if you have any second homes, you may decide to sell them or a business you own.

This will then release a large amount of liquid cash that you can use to top up your bucket again for you to spend.

You see, if planned correctly, your bucket is always being topped up. When you are young and working hard, any income you have or income from a 2nd job, your bucket is being filled up with your current income of wages and 2nd jobs or anything you can save, but if you time it right, then when you are older and decide to slow down, you can replace your income with something else like pensions or top it up with large amounts of money from selling a home or business you have.

Do not forget!

House prices typically double every ten years; there could be a severe amount of cash sitting in your home from when you bought it that you can release to help you later on.

This sounds great, doesn't it?

Based on what you have read, by planning correctly in advance, your bucket may not overflow but it will allow you to keep it topped up over time.

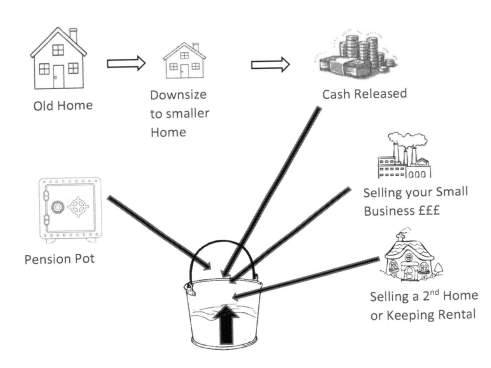

Old Home

Downsize to smaller Home

Cash Released

Pension Pot

Selling your Small Business £££

Selling a 2nd Home or Keeping Rental

This looks great, doesn't it?

But it is not quite that simple, and there are some other factors you must also consider, and we will cover this now.

CHAPTER 8

Your Outflowing Costs.

Your Outflowing Costs

Let's imagine that we now fit three taps to the bottom of your bucket.

Tap No. 1

Tap 1
Current.

This I have called your current lifestyle tap because it represents the outflows (costs) from your bucket that allow you to have your current lifestyle.

For example, you may have two cars, your children go to school, and you have clubs to pay for. You may go out a lot or have sports or hobbies that you participate in; holidays you go on. All this requires money, and for the moment, you must make sure that this money flowing out of tap one doesn't exceed what is inflowing into the bucket.

Tap No.2

When you retire, tap one gets turned off, and you open the second tap. This taps outflow represents the life you will lead in your retirement, to do all the things you always wanted to do while you are still active and could do. For example, the kids have got their own lives now, and you both want to explore the world and go back to where you were together before you had children, maybe spend your time going on cruises or just doing what the hell you want without kids now.

At last, you both have the time to do what you want. You are free! There is no work or job to go to, and your time is your own!!

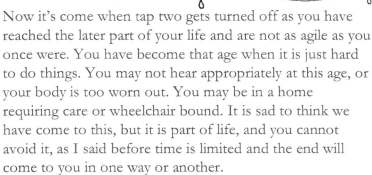

Tap 3 (Remaining Days)

Now it's come when tap two gets turned off as you have reached the later part of your life and are not as agile as you once were. You have become that age when it is just hard to do things. You may not hear appropriately at this age, or your body is too worn out. You may be in a home requiring care or wheelchair bound. It is sad to think we have come to this, but it is part of life, and you cannot avoid it, as I said before time is limited and the end will come to you in one way or another.

At this point in your life, your expenses will be more about just being comfortable; you want to be warm and fed and have the best care you can. By this age, you do not want to have to be worrying about money; this is why we are going through the information together so you will not need to. With careful planning, you can now enjoy the life ahead of you because the next stage from here is...

Things to remember:

- The money you have in your bucket is money you can spend on anything you want at any time, and we call it a liquid asset.
- Things like your home, a business, or a holiday home are not liquid unless they provide you with a regular income. They become liquid only when you sell them off to pocket the cash.
- These secondary sources of income can be sold when you need them to top up your bucket at a certain point in your life, or to BOOST it.
- Cash coming into your bucket like wages will one day stop, and new ones like a pension draw-down will take their place as an income, so you need to time them correctly when one stops and one starts, so you do not have a period where you have no money coming in.
- The three taps are your three stages of life, and the outflows or cash required for you to enjoy each stage of life at these points will vary.

After the 3rd tap, you know where the next stop is…

There is no escape for any of us!

Remember That.

CHAPTER 9

Protecting Your Bucket

Protecting Your Bucket

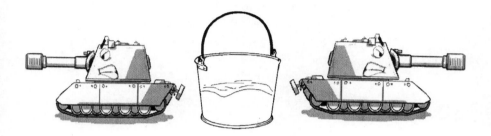

How do you protect the money in your bucket, so you have enough to last you till the end of your life?

The basics of this are that you will either have one of three things.

- You will have enough money to last you your lifetime.
- Your money will run out before you die (a big issue)
- You die leaving too much in the bucket, which, as discussed earlier, does not benefit you but benefits the government, who will rob you of your hard-earned money.

1. **If you have enough money**, fantastic! you will have a great life. You have worked hard, so now enjoy it.

2. **If your bucket runs early**, then this is a significant problem. Chances are you have worked all your life, but if you cannot do the things you always wanted to because you don't have the money then what is the point?
This is the reason we are going through this together now.

The idea is that with the proper education, you can correctly exercise and control your finances and from there, plan and forecast your future. To avoid this before it even has a chance, we want you to have the funds to enjoy your life. It is not that difficult a problem to get around. The basics are that you need to either increase the money coming into your bucket or consider reducing your outgoings.

This sounds like pretty basic advice, but the fact is that most people are in this situation. By having the education to work through this in advance and facing up to some truths that you cannot buy the latest iPhone, because the one you bought last month *is* good enough, you can avoid this situation. You need to plan to ensure your bucket doesn't run out.

3. **When you die, are you are leaving too much in the bucket?**

This, I find is **the saddest issue,**

Why is this, you ask?

Because it means that you have died, leaving a large amount of money. Congratulations on trying to take it with you.

So let me put it this way, you have worked your ass off through life; everything you have bought you have paid tax for; you've paid it on food, fuel, clothes, holidays, and stamp duty on your home. If you pass things down to other people, this is taxed as it is treated as a benefit. Even if you gift your children money to help them in life, it will get taxed somewhere along the line.

So, we are going to work through this step by step, so you can plan to spend it on the things you want to and enjoy your life. If it also allows you to make sure the value of your estate is reduced to keep death taxes to a minimum.

Why work till you're 65 if you've worked so hard that you have the money to take it easy from 45? That's another 20 years of travelling or doing what you love, and we can walk you through this; otherwise, the next step is…

Now you're dead!
You've left too much money in your bucket, so before it gets passed down to loved ones, the Tax Man is first in line and will take (at this time of writing) a whopping 40% of your money as tax, and they will not even thank you, but they will charge your children interest on the money if they don't give it to them on time!

This, I find, is nothing more than theft. You paid tax when you earnt it initially. To me, the worst is that when you were alive, you DID NOT do enough things or enjoy life while you were on this planet.

Imagine if you had the ability after you were dead to be able to watch from the sky as the tax man takes 40% of what you left in your bucket, you would probably be turning in your grave as you could have done so much more with *YOUR* money when you were alive, but you didn't & now you have given it to them to fund whatever new schemes the government thinks up. You could have had so many more experiences and shared them with people you love or even given them away to charity, but you decided to keep it, and now it's too late; it's the government's money now.

This may sound harsh, but I need you to understand the basics of what will happen if you die and leave money behind.

But you are reading this book at the right time; together we can plan for your future before these events happen. The game aims to leave as little as possible to the government when you die.

The old school mentality was to work till 65, retire to a life well earnt and draw your government pension.

The fact is that the retirement age will be increasing to 67 by 2028 and rising. Your state pension will not be enough to live off with the cost of living in the UK & the government will not look after you in your old age if you have over £14,000 in assets. You will have to sell them to pay for your care home, so why have a fortune tied up in your home?

You may as well spend it and have debt, as your government can't tax a debt but that's another subject you can contact us about.

What if you do have enough money?

Most people don't even know about having a central place where all their money is put, I'm not talking about a bank account but referring to the analogy of the bucket.

If no one has ever shown you or explained the theory that we have covered, then these people tend to work week to week, not enjoying their life to the full, when really they could be turning opportunities for adventure or travelling away blindly and working full time when they could be spending it on having a great time making memories or having the freedom to at least reduce their hours and maybe do a 3 day week.

Do you know how much money you need to have the choice to stop working and have the life you want?

Will you be okay?

Have you saved enough for your future?

Again, we will take you through the process, so you can see your £ or $ amount number and decide if you are ready now or when you will be at that position in life to do what you want.

You must take these steps now to make sure that you look after yourself in the future!

CHAPTER 10

Don't wait to be saved!

Don't wait to be saved!

Please do not rely on suddenly winning the lottery or getting an inheritance from a parent or someone to sort out your future magically.
While it would be great to receive a cash injection and I hope you are lucky in winning extra funds, do not rely on it.
Also do not completely rely on selling your home in the future to pull out the equity to help you get out of trouble, you need to plan your finances for the future first.

Again, while selling your home can be extremely helpful, please do not rely on this, as there could be outside your-control factors, like a recession that may devalue what you thought it was worth, or quite simply, you may decide it's your family home, and you don't want to sell it.

How much money do I need for the future?

Where do I start?

If asked, most people don't know the answer to how much they really need, everyone is different, they may fire out a strangely large sum like "I need 5 million pounds!" but they don't know the accurate figure and how to calculate how they would figure this out.

Simply the best place to start is where you are now in your life.

In one column, you can put down all your liquid assets (cash you can get your hands on quickly), so this is the amount of money going into your bucket. Then you can put a list of your outflows into another column (rent, electric, gas, food, internet costs, mobile phone costs, etc.) so you know exactly how much it costs you to live your life right now in your current lifestyle, but your expenses should not be more than 80% of your income.

Simply put; if you are not bringing in enough money for 80% of your income to cover the costs of your expenses, then you need to either earn more or you need to either increasing your worth and get a raise, get a second job, or finding another way of making more money,

No, it's not impossible!

Let me put it this way, I'm already going in a positive direction and I've left the saying " I can't do it"….way behind me and you should do the same and the people who also make comments like this to you, the point of the Future Forecast Planner is that we are moving away from the way of life you bare currently in and into a new one, so sacrifices will need to be made.

You may also need to look at subtracting things like, your new TV package, that expensive new mobile phone you now want or other luxuries that, quite frankly, you cannot afford. Remember these are luxuries and not necessities.
As an example, get a pen, paper and a calculator.....
Do you have online services? Netflix, Amazon, Paramount, Disney etc.? do you really need all of them?

Take your least favourite one, how much do you pay for it for a month? Write it down then multiply that by 12 to give you a yearly cost, then multiply that by 35 the average working adult life, how much have you just saved yourself by getting rid of something you don't use a lot?

Remember, your bills must be covered by 60% of your income. WHY?... Do you say?
This is because you need the 40% to be able to invest or use it to save and increase the volume of your bucket for your future and this amount will compound overtime to create wealth for your future.

To help you grow your wealth we are going to use a model.

The 60/20/20 Rule

The 60/20/20 is a rule is where your bills must be no more than 60% of your income and must cover all of your bills. If you have problems making this work, then I suggest you contact me to get some more advice and help on this matter, but until then creating a simple budget and planner will help a great deal.

The next 20% is your spending for the things you want to do right now, you need to create a separate savings account and pay this 20% into it, you will be amazed how quickly it will build up and by the end of the year you will have a pot with enough to do something you really want to do like go on a holiday.

With the remaining 20% you also put this into another saving account and do not touch it that is for you to build up and then use the money to put into investments or placing it into something that will create an income, slowly invest into this and don't touch it! over time this will compound and you will be wealthy, but to get there first you must create and stick to a plan and have a good mindset, this can be taught to you quite easily.

If you don't have the discipline and self-control to do this you may find yourself in trouble later on, and if you can't stick to the 60/20/20 rule then you may find out later on that you were just working week to week to pay your bills and end up staying in the position where you are right now, it's all about discipline, this is why most people never get out of the cycle, it's all down to budgeting, planning, self-control and for you to know it won't be easy, but nothing worthwhile ever is and together we can break this cycle for you.

I will reiterate this again!

You MUST create self-discipline and if you don't have self-discipline then you will never progress from this point where you are right now in your life, you must take yourself from this point you find yourself in and create a long term plan to be where you want to be in years to come, this is not a get rich quick system but a get wealthy slowly system.

If however to start with you find your bills are higher than expected and you really can't get all this paid by the 60% even after sacrificing some things, then if you have to tweak the numbers to say 80/10/10 this is not a failure…this is good on you that you are following a system…obviously it will take longer but you have already made the 1st step that so many others simply can't be bothered to do, then over time if you feel you can do this you can increase the figure up to 60/20/20 .

Set up a separate bank account & never spend from it.

Step 1:
When you receive any money for wages or things that generate cash for you, set up a rule to transfer 20% if you can into this new account, your money goes into it like a pension pot, and you adjust your life to live off the remaining 80%.

The rule is…That you never withdraw any money from this account it is for your investments only so name this account '**Investments**'.

You only use it to put in 20% of your income and let it build up over time to a point where you can then use this money for your investments so they can grow passive income for you (we will cover this later!) So, when your funds/ wages, or any form of other income gets depsited into your main bank account, then make sure 20% gets transferred into the new account called 'Investments'.

Step 2:
When your life has adjusted and you have become comfortable that 20% of your income goes into the investments account that you don't touch, then create another account, one for another 20% and this you can name 'holiday fund'. This account you can put in 20% or start at 10% but again do not touch this and look into it at the end of the year to see how much it grows to, this account can be used as the only account you use to buy the luxuries in life or holidays.
Simple put if the money isn't in it then you don't spend it.

Increasing your worth to increase your income.

As mentioned earlier, I said I would briefly cover this, as it is a big subject to cover in-depth, and we will be more than happy to help you (if you need help, get in contact with us by our email at the end of this book) but we will keep this example as basic as we can.

Years ago, the only way you could advertise for work was by the newspaper, cards in shop windows or by calling someone, BUT what a fantastic world we live in now!!! You can advertise on Facebook, Instagram, YouTube, and much more, and the great thing is THEY'RE FREE! You can work a regular job and earn from home in the evening! People will pay you for your knowledge, and you can monetize what you know very easy now on various forms of digital media.

There are so many opportunities now; there is absolutely no reason you cannot make a side hustle and get extra income if you want to.

I myself have spent a lot of years running multiple businesses and making many mistakes as I progressed slowly along the path, many of these mistakes I have learnt from and promised never to repeat again and some I have again as I sometimes forget and need to be taught a lesson again, but because I constantly push forward with drive and self-control my experience has grown, believe me I'm far from perfect, but because of self-discipline, I have now been able to progress far from where I first started all those years ago to where I am now and what I offer is my personal knowledge and experience that has cost me so much finically and mentally to get from where I was, to where I am now where I am now in a position that I can offer this advice and help new business owners and people who want to better themselves, to obtain the next level and I do this for 2 reasons:

1. To offer advice to gain an extra income for my family.

2. So I can help these people not make the same expensive mistakes I made, thus saving them thousands and you can do the same to with your knowledge.

NEVER depend on a single income!

Your knowledge is an extra or potential future income, from those who WILL PAY for information they don't possess...

Don't forget that!

Use your talents & skills that you would generally use for free just because you love what you do and learn to make money from them.

Let's say you're good at cooking or maybe your good at sports or playing computer games or surfing etc...

Learn to monetize these amazing skills that you naturally have and use them to show others your secrets and tips of how you do it, but don't do it for free...

Sell this information to create a second income for yourself."

For example:
You're really good at cooking and your friends always complement you about how great it tastes....
Maybe it's the perfect omelette!

Then why not create a video of how you do it step by step and put this online and charge a token amount.

If you have any questions or want to learn how to do this, then use the email address on the website.

Learn the system described here and then if you would like us to help you then get in contact and we will be happy to help you in this journey.

CHAPTER 11

Planning Your Future

Planning your future

Are you ready to start planning your future?

What you will need now is to sit down with a notepad or large A3 paper, packs of multi-coloured pens, a ruler and a calculator, I hope you are good at maths as this is going to take quite a bit of time, as you also need to be able to work out interest rates that need to be applied as well as its opposite end of decreasing money or inflation and this needs to be plotted over time. You will need to complete a series of complex calculation for every year of your life and make sure the maths are correct otherwise you won't get your correct answer.
If at any point your situation changes then you will need to completely rework the entire charts and calculations again for every year, are you ready for me to explain how to do this?

Or does this completely turn you off the idea?

If so, then how would you feel if we did all that work for you, we literally would number crunch all the data for you in our custom made 'Future Forecast' system just for this purpose.

Our team have spent thousands of hours working with programmers, financial advisors, and web designers to create a program where you can input your data into the various boxes that are clearly marked, so you can see what your financial future looks like. its unique and only for you, we have spared no expense on designing this system, the programme is fully encrypted, and you are the only one with access to it, no one else will have or be able to see your data, when you are ready you can also download the data as a pdf, so you have a physical copy too.

We have split the various stages for the Future Forecast section down into separate screens, so it's a simple process of entering the data in 1 page and when you're ready to move on, you click on the button and move to the next page, we have spent a great deal of time making this simple for you to use.

Every page has an option where you can click on the video section and we will walk you through that page you are on, step by step, all you must do is watch the video for that page then simply copy the process using your own numbers, each video is only a few minutes long. It's effortless to use.

But the best bit is, that if you need a break, then whenever you log back in with your own unique username and password (that you will create) your data will still be there when you need it, so at any time, day or night, you can log in and tweak the information or just update it, then print out a new pdf to keep it current, if you get a raise or extra income, then simply alter the figure, if you have a setback and something happens thats takes money away from you, just enter the data and the system will adjust and display the new data in a form of an image to show how this has impacted your target, so you can make a plan before in advance.

The purpose of this system is that you can see how much money you need to live the life you need, and like a fortune teller, so you can see what your cash future will look like and make sure you don't end up with too much money in your bank account when you die.

If the end figure is too high then great, don't worry , it simply means you can then reverse engineer your life and increase the spending when your younger, so you have more to spend on adventures or passing down to people you love and as you enter these values the graphs will change to reflect what this will do for your life, so you can adjust and readjust as much as you want.

Remember, the perfect result is you have a unique, fantastic life doing the things you want, and on the day of your death, you have nothing left in your account unless you want there to be.

We are not leaving your future up to chance!

So, for the first time, you will be able to see what is in your bucket at different stages in your life, shown in years and hopefully give you some absolute clarity of where you are heading in life.

If you have too much money, then spend it and adjust the graph, if you need to make savings, then adjust the graph, if you get an extra job and have more income, adjust the graph, it's easy to use and will change the way you view your life if seen this way.

Image if you could give up work years earlier than you thought, wouldn't that be amazing to see if you have that opportunity?

We really want to help educate as many people as possible with this system and give you the tools to plan for financial freedom!

This program will change how you see things for your future, it's all laid out in a simple-to-see chart. The sole purpose of this system is to help you plan for your future. I don't want you going through life worrying about it.

It will help show any traps or warnings before they happen. This way, you will have the time to spot them and then plan for this point in advance to avoid them altogether.

Life is to be lived!

Do not...

Be an enslaved person for the rest of your life worrying about your finances and stuck in jobs you don't like, if you hate your job that much, then change it for something you enjoy or love, then the money you make from that can be entered into the program to see how this will affect your life.

Imagine if you quit your job and did something you really wanted to do or loved to do then imagine having a system that showed you that the money you make from this new venture was enough for your future, wouldn't that be amazing to do your perfect job and know it can pay the bills and create a future for you?

Wouldn't this be perfect?

Chances are some of you reading this are ready to change your life. Still, the uncertainty stops you from undertaking and completing this change, the what-if question, but this program will allow you to see your future in a couple of hours and save you tens of years bouncing off the sides like a ball in a pin ball machine, just input this data for your perfect job before you do it in the real world, so you can see if it's worthwhile doing.

I get paid for something I love to do and it's not writing books, I am doing this as I want to help others to get on the same path I use every day, but the unfortunate fact is that most people do not do this.

They stay in a job they hate, but they don't hate it enough to be able to tell their boss to shove it & leave!

Therefore, they stay stuck in that shit job, day after day, working for years. Maybe they will have a bit of savings when they retire at 65 or maybe they won't, they just don't know, but if they end up losing their job, then a major decision has now been made for them.

PLEASE

Don't let this be you!

**The fear of being stuck in
A never-ending cycle.**

- Wake up exhausted.
- Eat breakfast.
- Go to a job you don't like.
- Work hard for a wage helping the boss achieve their dreams & not my own, when they buy nice cars or go on holiday.
- Go home.
- Eat tea.
- Repeat day after day.
- Count the days till I have time off for a holiday that puts me in more debt.
- Repeat this yearly cycle for 40 plus years till I retire or die.

Our goal as mentioned in this book numerous times is to get this information out to educate as many people as we can, we truly believe that this will help many people who were never taught the basics of a money mindset or a future forecaster.

Look at it as being taught to drive a car by your old instructor with the handbrake on, everywhere you're going your pushing the accelerator to go faster while revving the hell out of the engine and just getting there slowly, then a new instructor helps you and with a little bit of new information, this person has told you how to press the button on the top of the handbrake to finally release it and now....

Vooooomm you're going to get moving in the direction you want to go, so much smoother, quicker and easier than you were before.

CHAPTER 12

 YOUR FUTURE FORECASTER

 **YOUR FUTURE FORECASTER**

This is the Ultimate Money Planner for you for the future and we have called the programme 'The Future Forecaster'.

Now because you took action to think really carefully and decide to make a change in your life by purchasing this book, I want to thank you very much for your support and helping us with our mission to get our Future Forecaster system out to as many people as we can, the pricing of the book was designed for this reason alone and chosen so we could cover our costs of printing and shipping to you, if you're wondering why we did this, well it's because I want to help as many people as I can with knowledge that I had passed down me so I can learn and pass it to you and hopefully you will also do the same and who knows, we just may start a community with enough members to help and support each other and be able to bounce off each other with new ideas. we are trying to create a bigger thing, by the collaborative power of group thinking.

Are you ready to transform your life and take a leap towards a brighter future?

Imagine having a powerful tool that will streamline your decision-making process that will provide invaluable insights, and help you make informed choices that will positively impact your life about your future finances.

With this new tool you will have the power to plan and chart your future with ease. No more guesswork or tedious calculations – our system does all the heavy lifting for you, saving you time and effort to get on and enjoy life.
You'll be able to confidently navigate through life's challenges, make strategic moves, and achieve your goals like never before.

Don't let fear or uncertainty hold you back. It's time to take charge of your life and make meaningful strides towards your dreams.

All you must do is scan the QR code or type in the web address on the following page to embrace the power of this life-changing software and embark on a journey towards a brighter future. Your best days are yet to come – let's make it happen together!

It will even allow you to make copies of your current situation, where you are now and run multiple versions of what you want to do, so you can choose the best path, then, if you like what you see you can just follow the plan that prints out.

The Future Forecaster software also will allow you to create custom plans for your friends, family and children, it's completely unlimited to you.

What I am offering you is an opportunity, and you must be able to identify this, then from here, you can either do nothing...... or take **'ACTION'** as you did when you decided to make the plunge and purchase this book, why did you do this? Hopefully it was because you want to move your life forward for the better.

So unlock the power of planning ahead with our cutting-edge system. Our Future Forecaster has helped countless individuals, including myself, make money adjustments to secure their financial future. Now, with the latest advancements in technology and processing power, we've created a fully digital version that can be accessed from anywhere in the world. Whether you want to use it sparingly or extensively, you can even create separate sections for each family member or allow your children to use it.

The data is presented in easy-to-follow graphics, making it simple to track and visualize your financial goals. Take the next step and visit our landing page to experience the convenience and flexibility of our modernized Future Forecaster system.

Are you happy where you are now?
or
Would you like to be given the tools to alter your future?

YOUR FUTURE FORECASTER

Take action now with just 5 minutes of your time!

The process is simple:

Step 1 : Scan the QR code or link with your phone camera

www.FutureForecaster.co.uk

Step 2: Watch the 60 second video

Step 3: Commit to taking action

That's it!

"Escape the Hamster Wheel:

Unlock Your Future with Our Proven Strategies!"

What's Keeping You Stuck?

Discover How to Overcome Barriers and Move Forward!"

Learn More at...

www.FutureForecaster.co.uk

OR

Simply scan the QR code with your phones camera.

You really do only have one life to live.

www.FutureForecaster.co.uk

Printed in Great Britain
by Amazon